RELAXING LANDSCAPES

adult coloring book

This book belongs to:

....

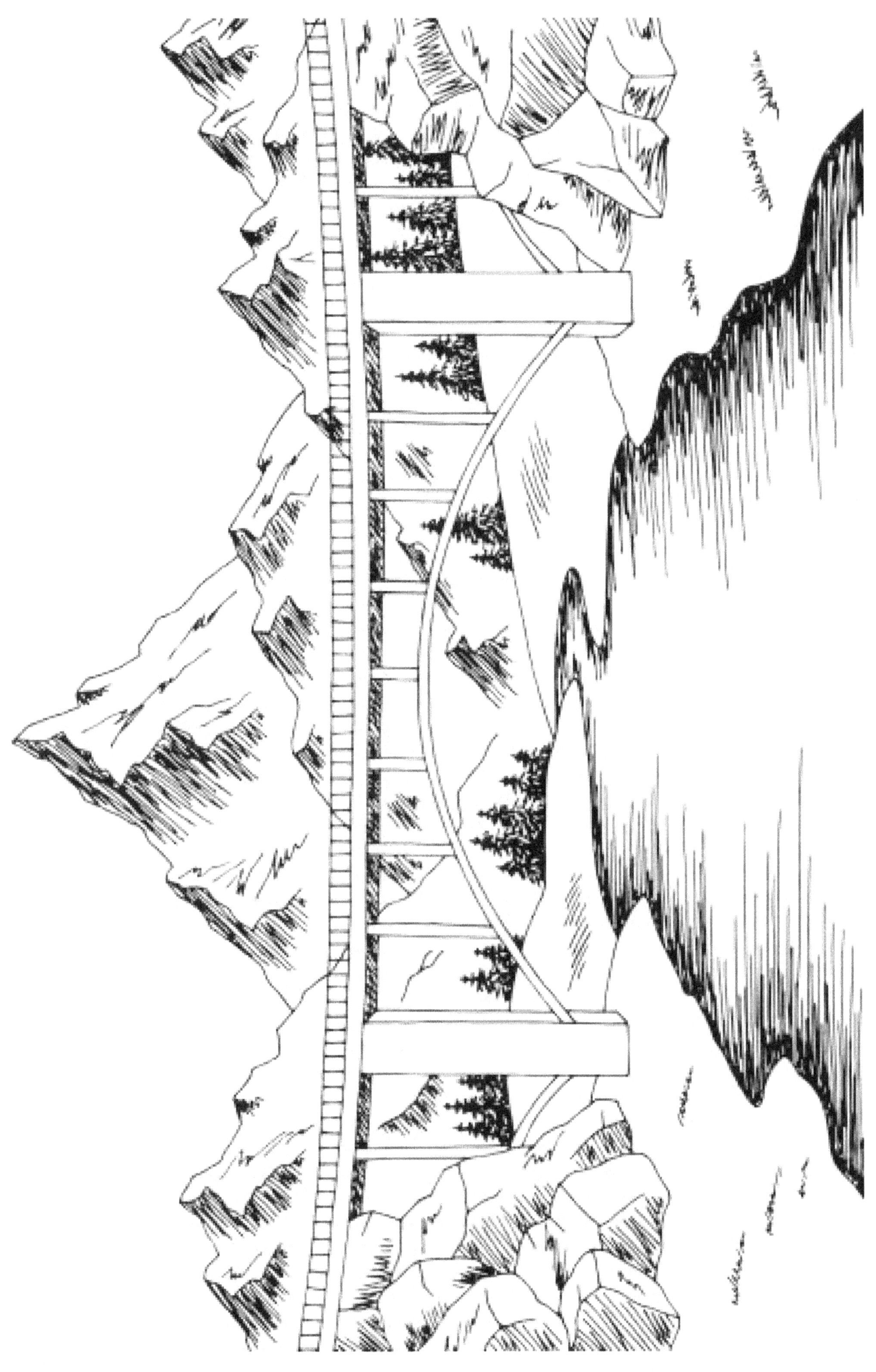

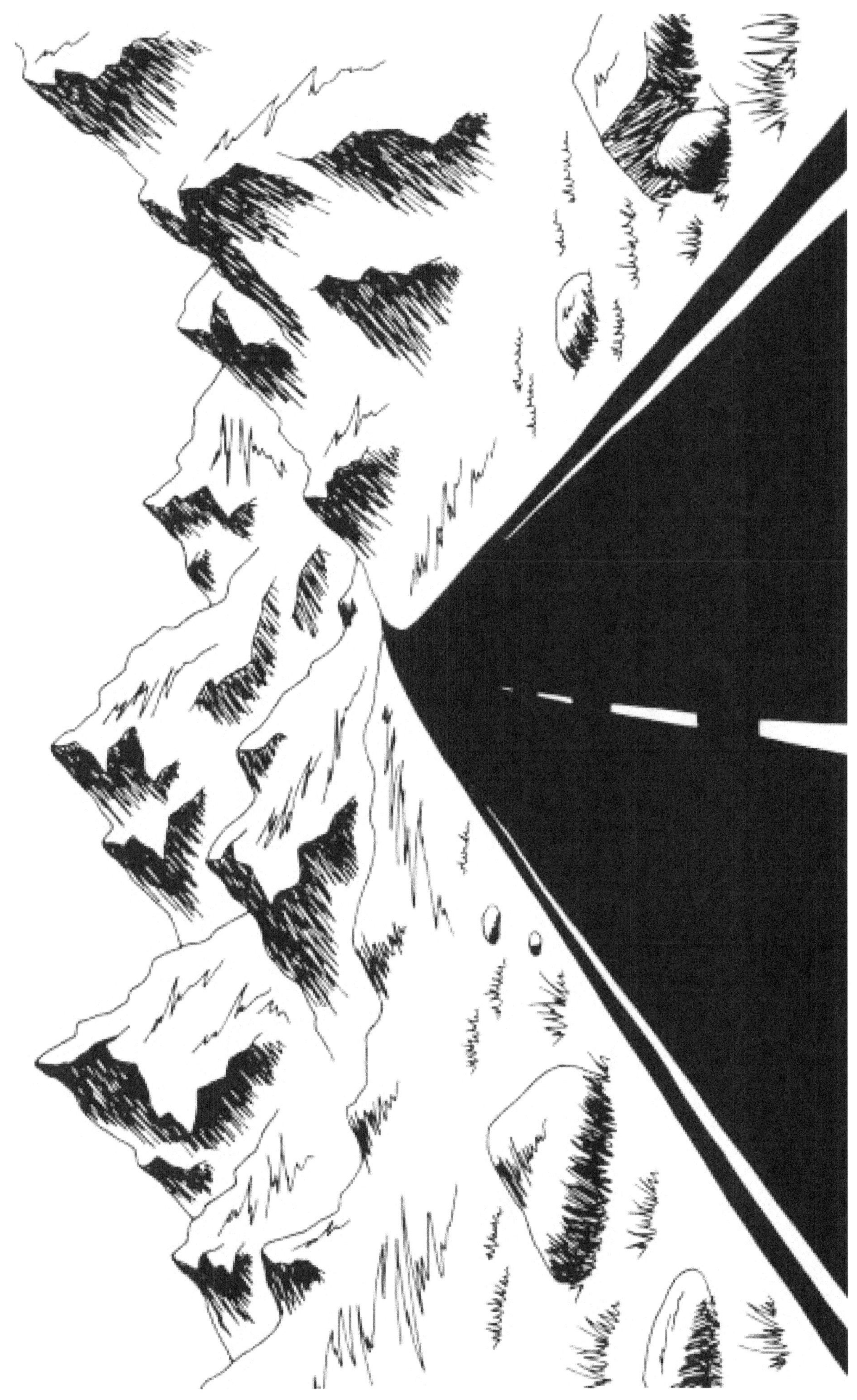

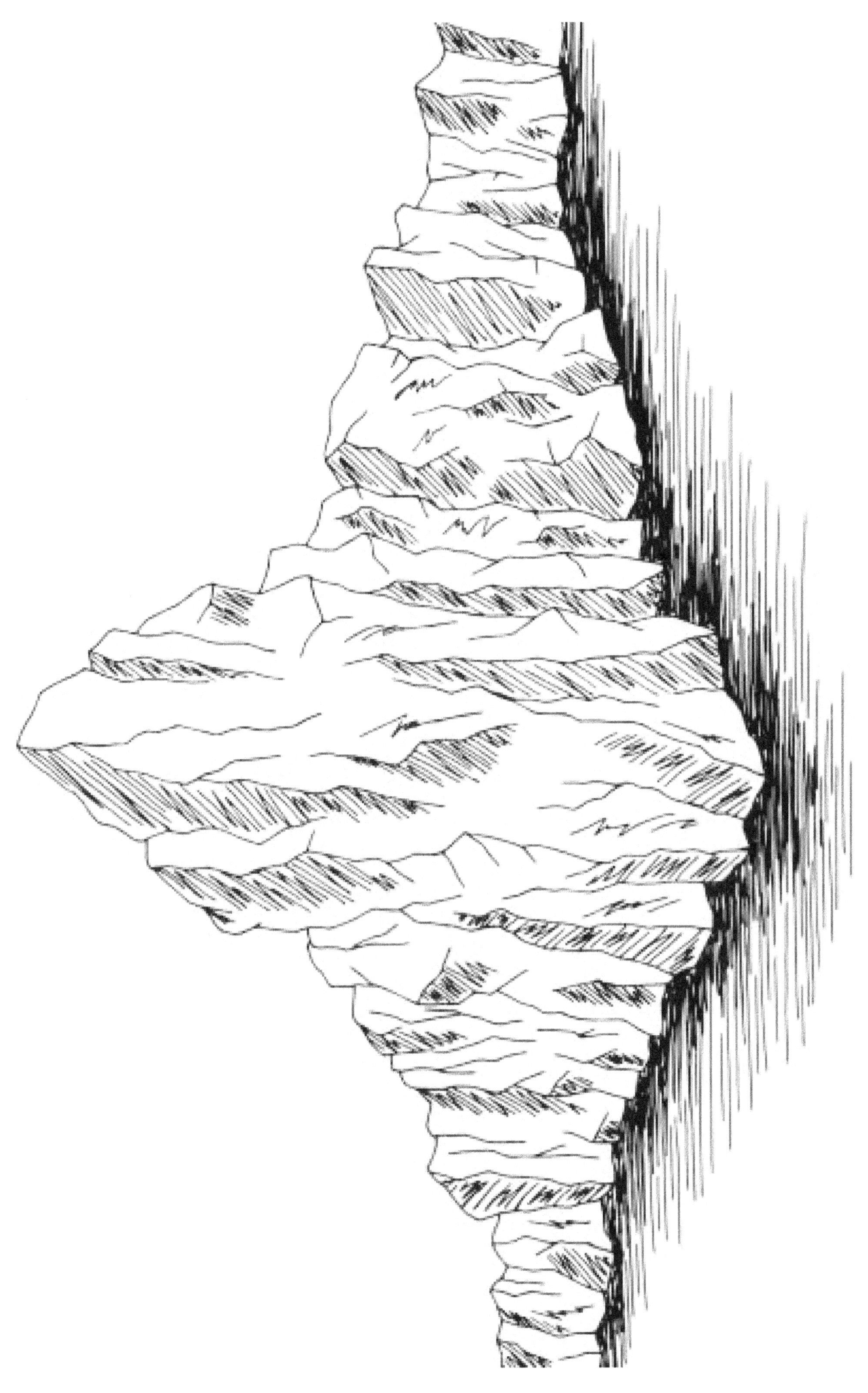

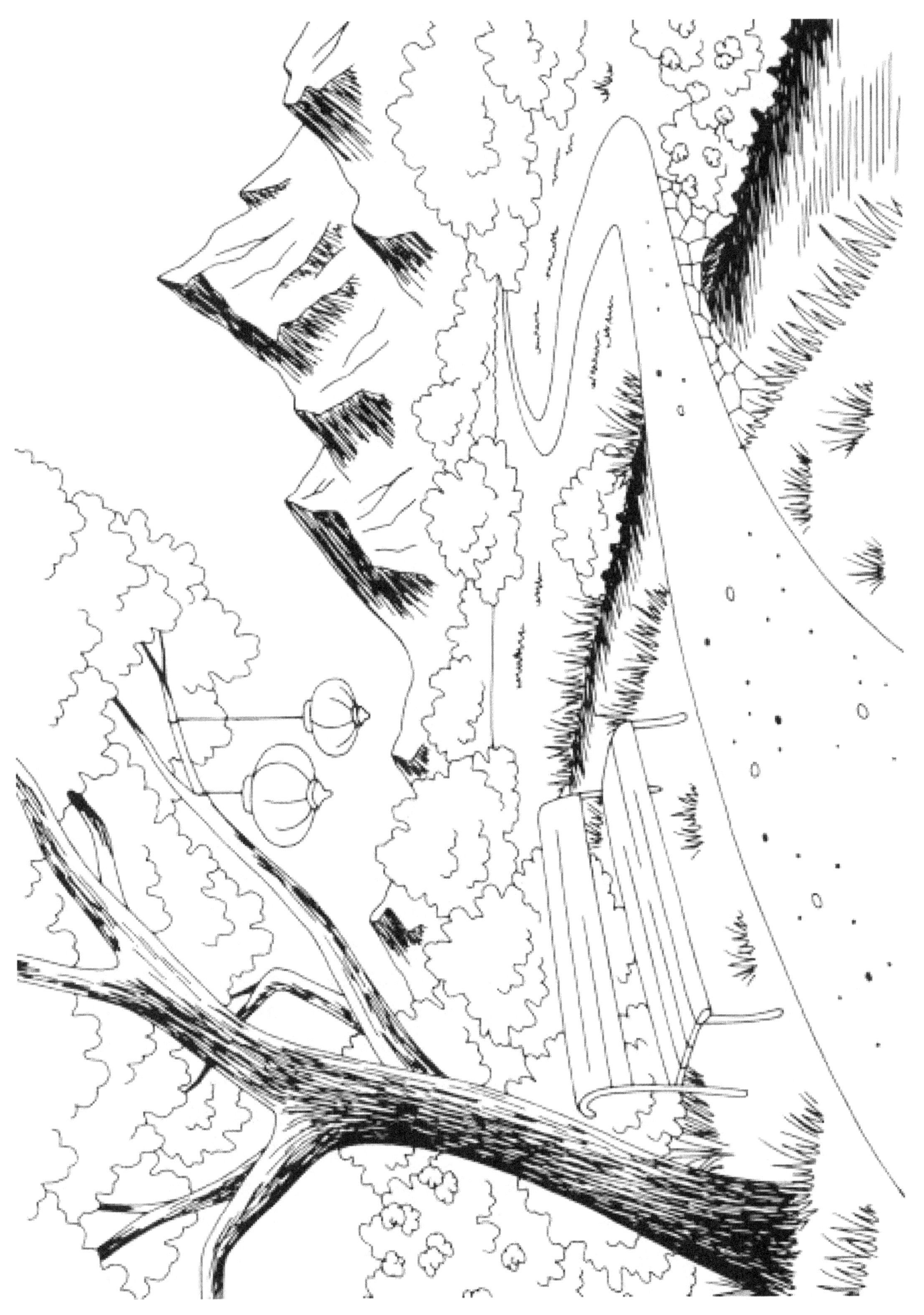

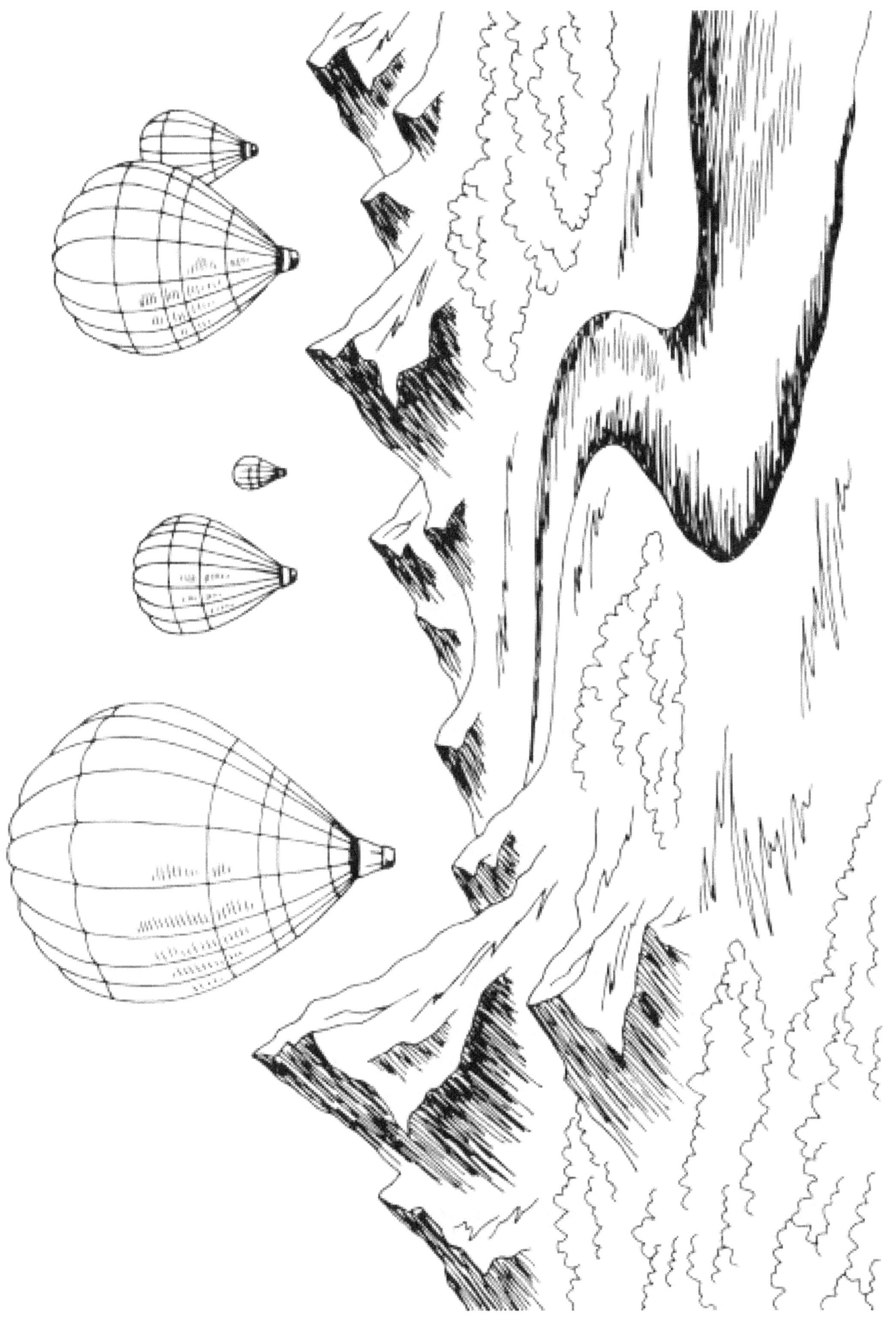

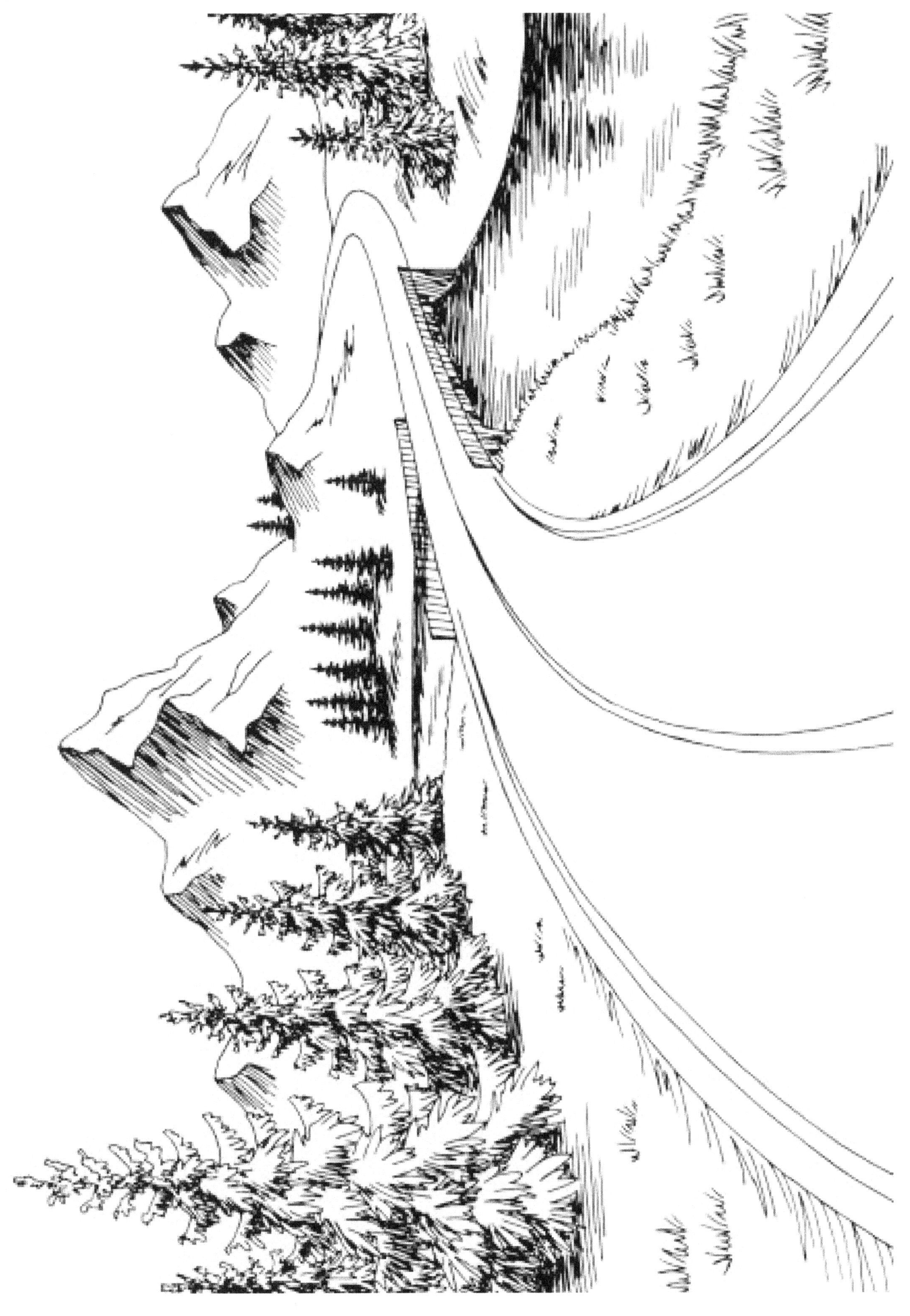

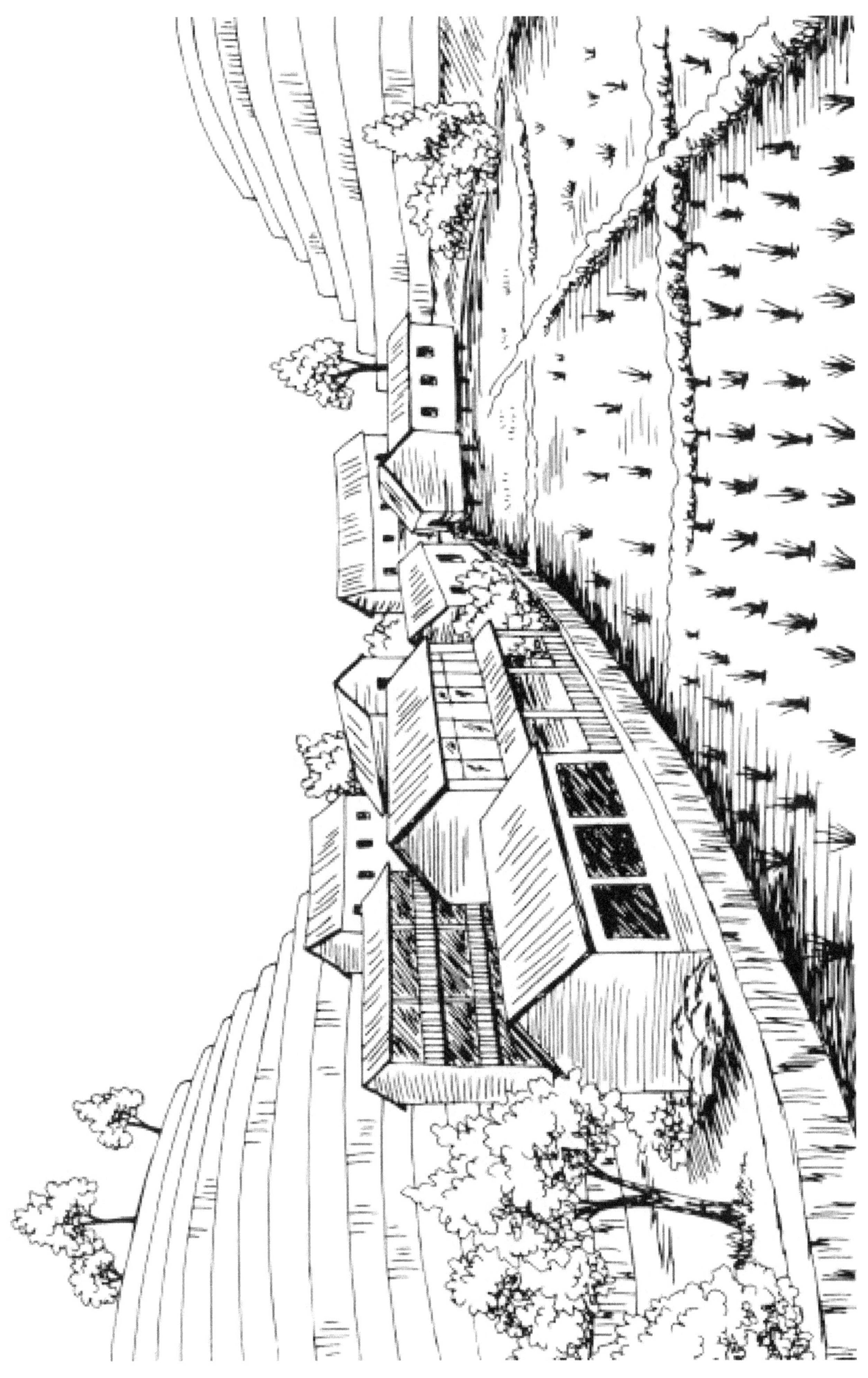

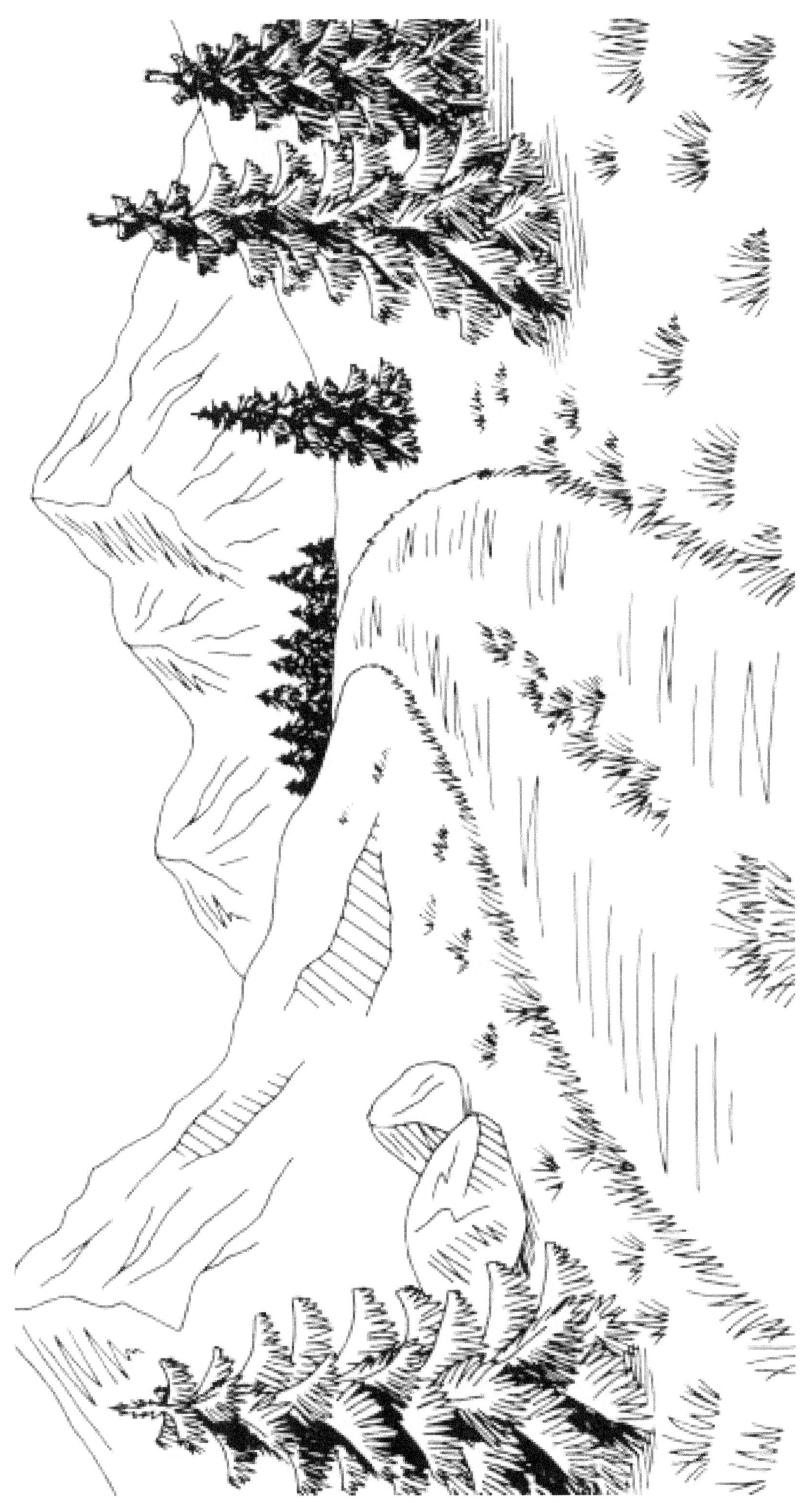

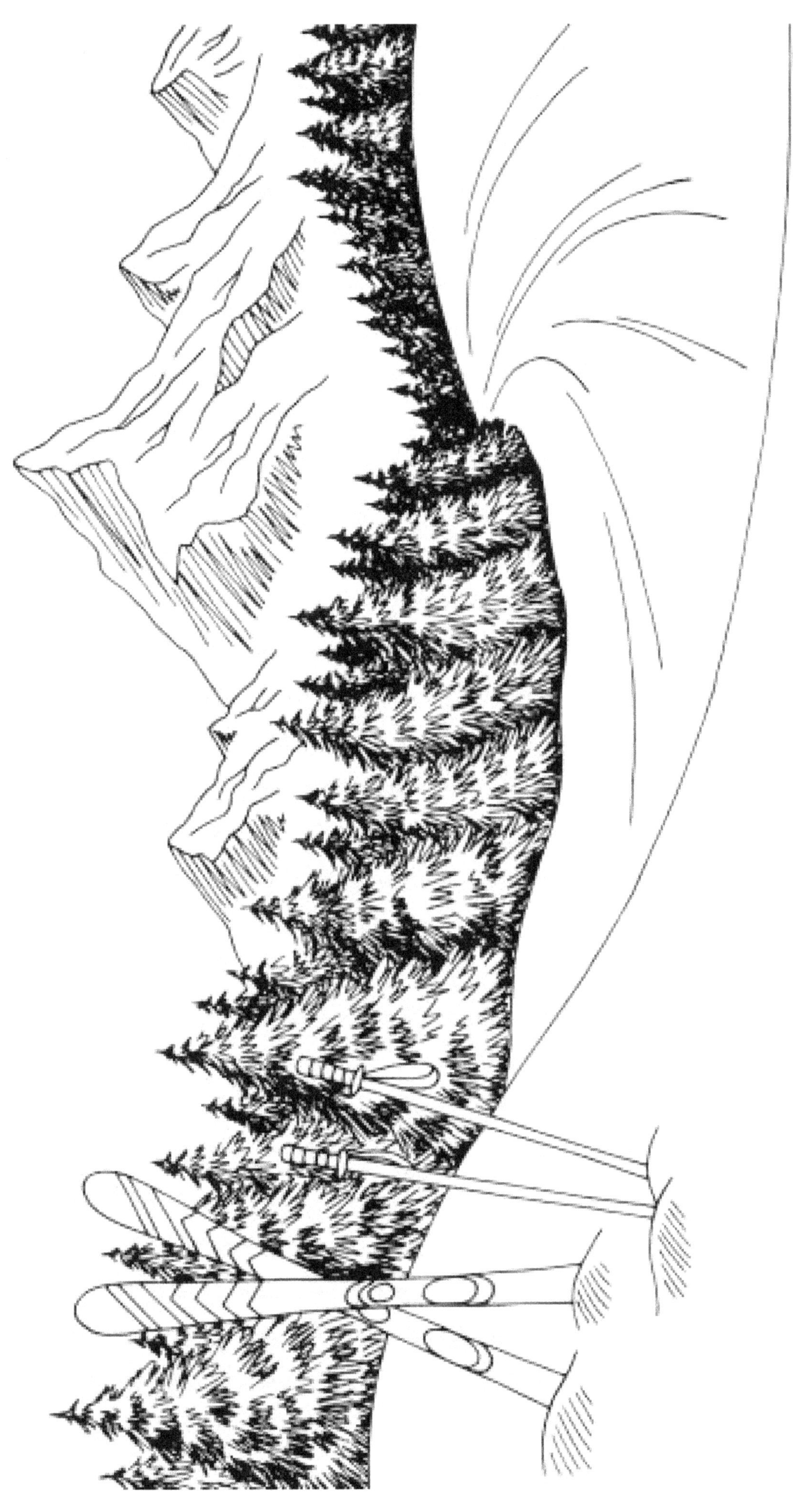

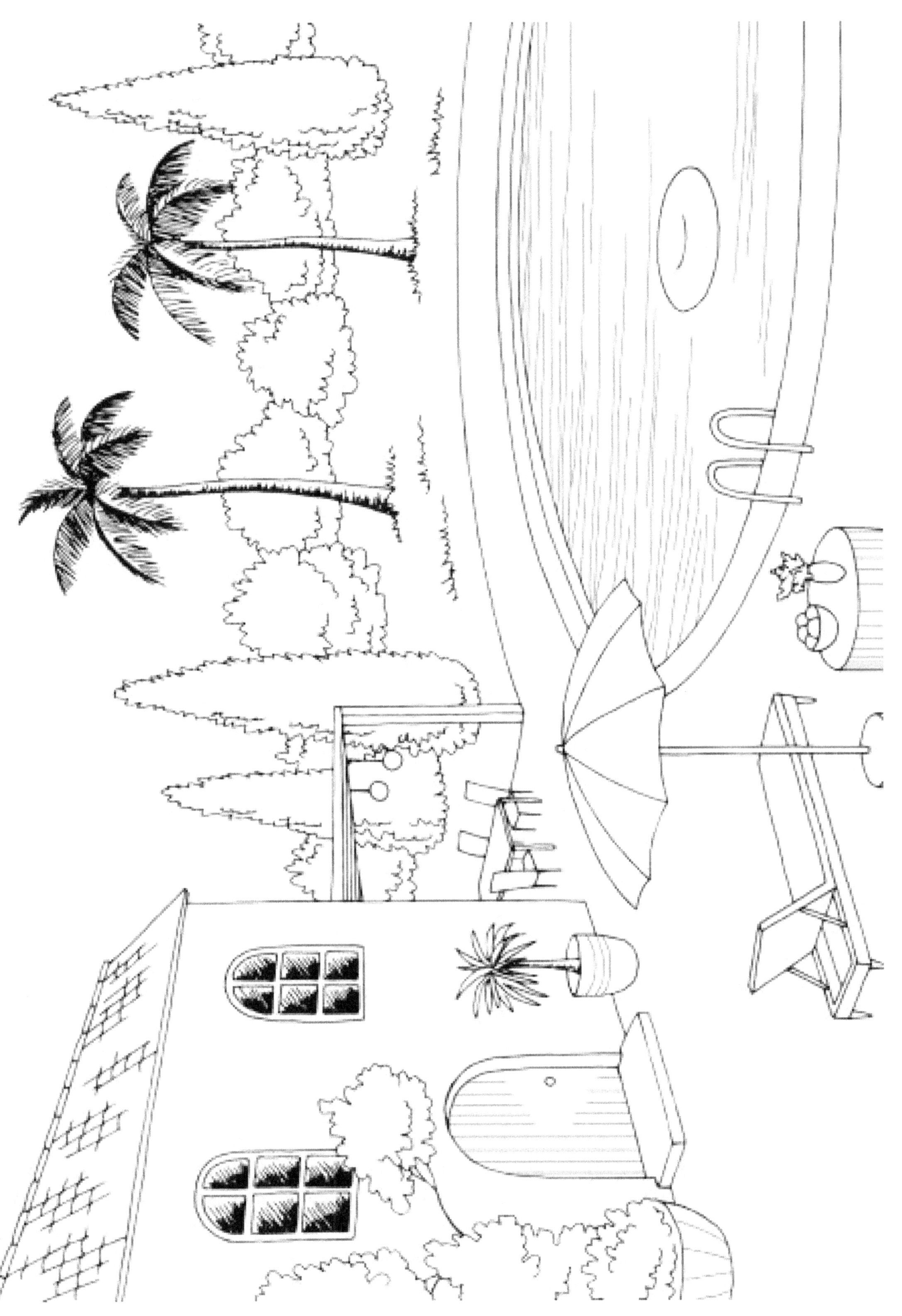

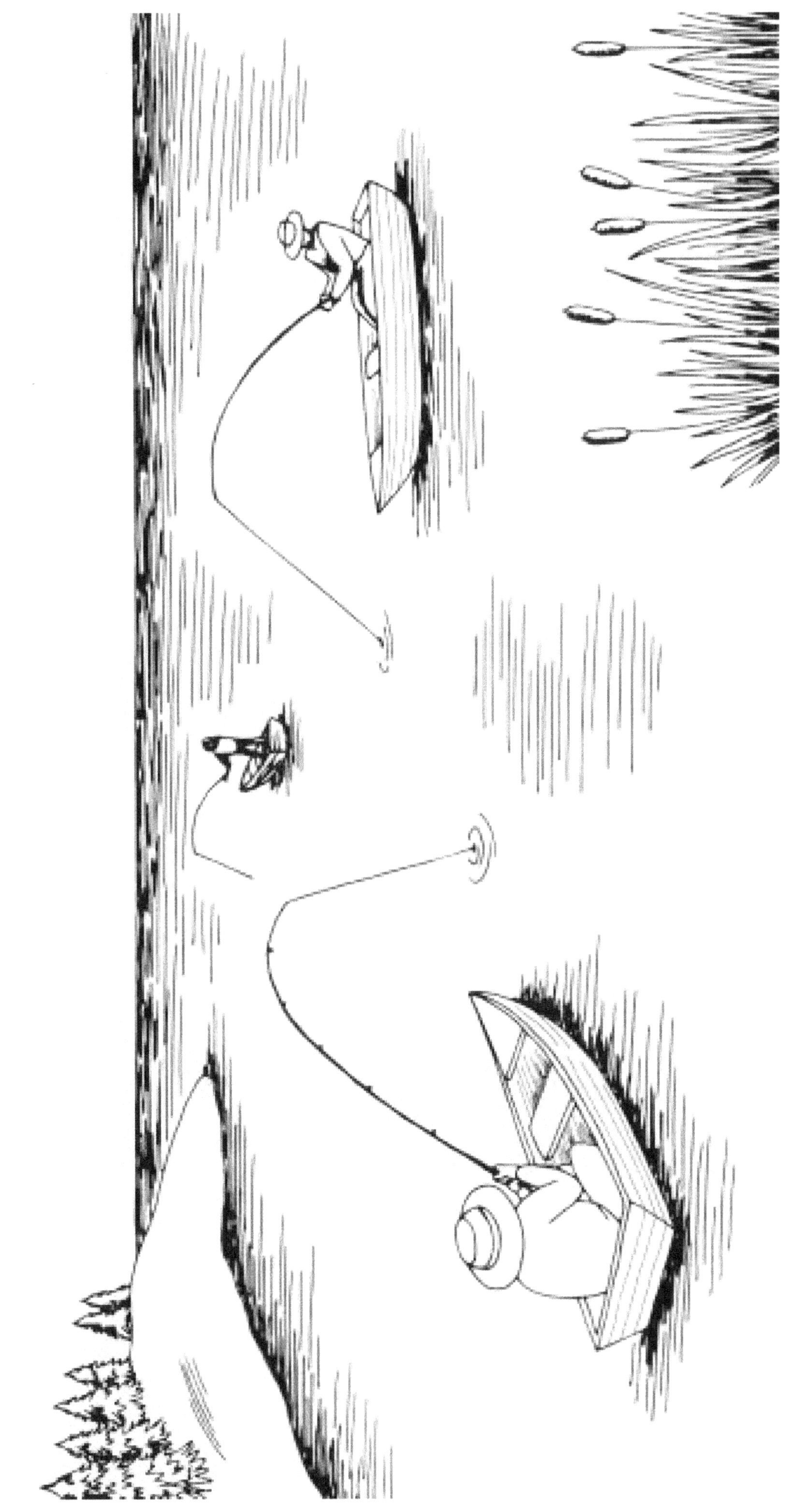

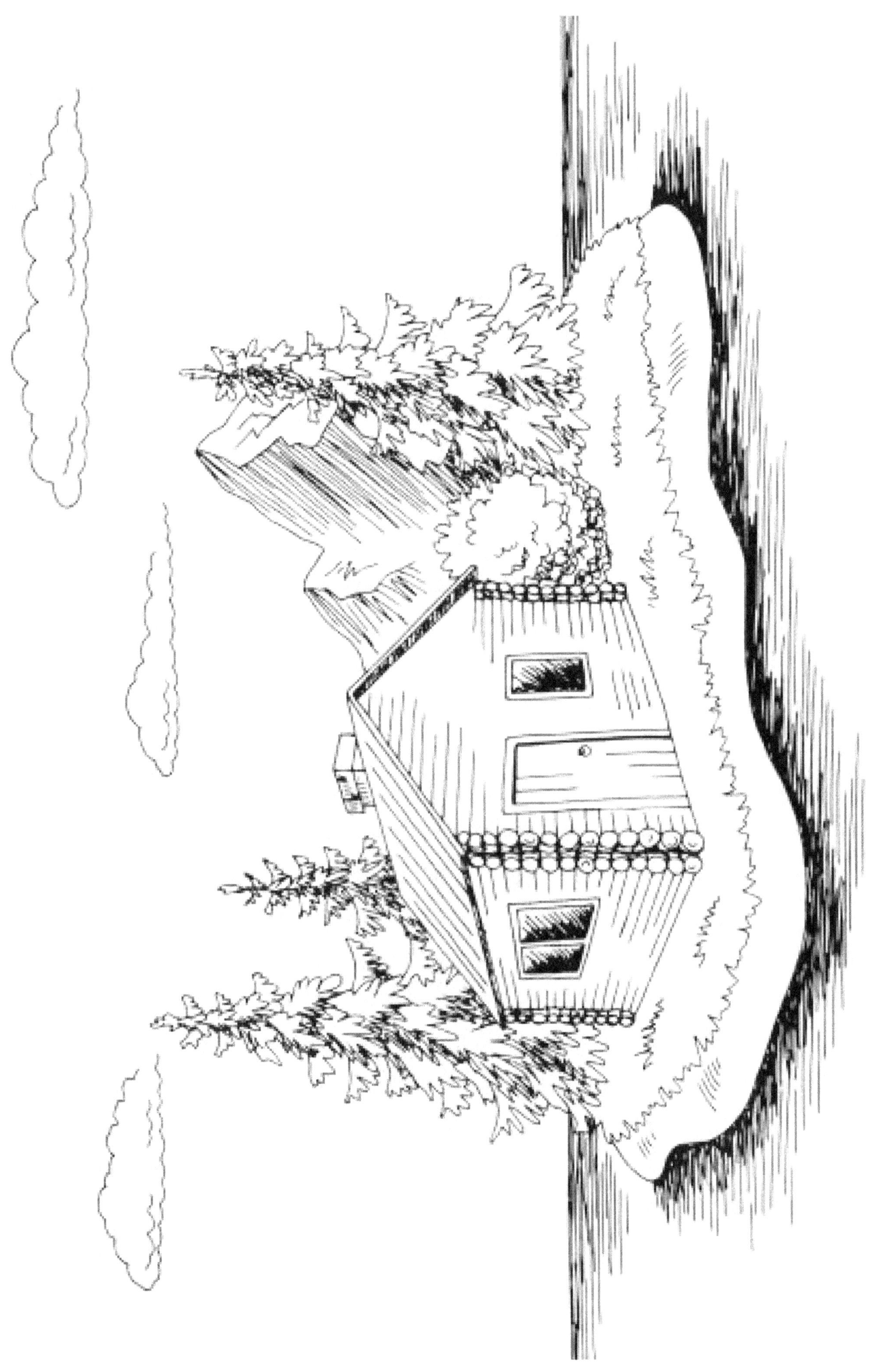

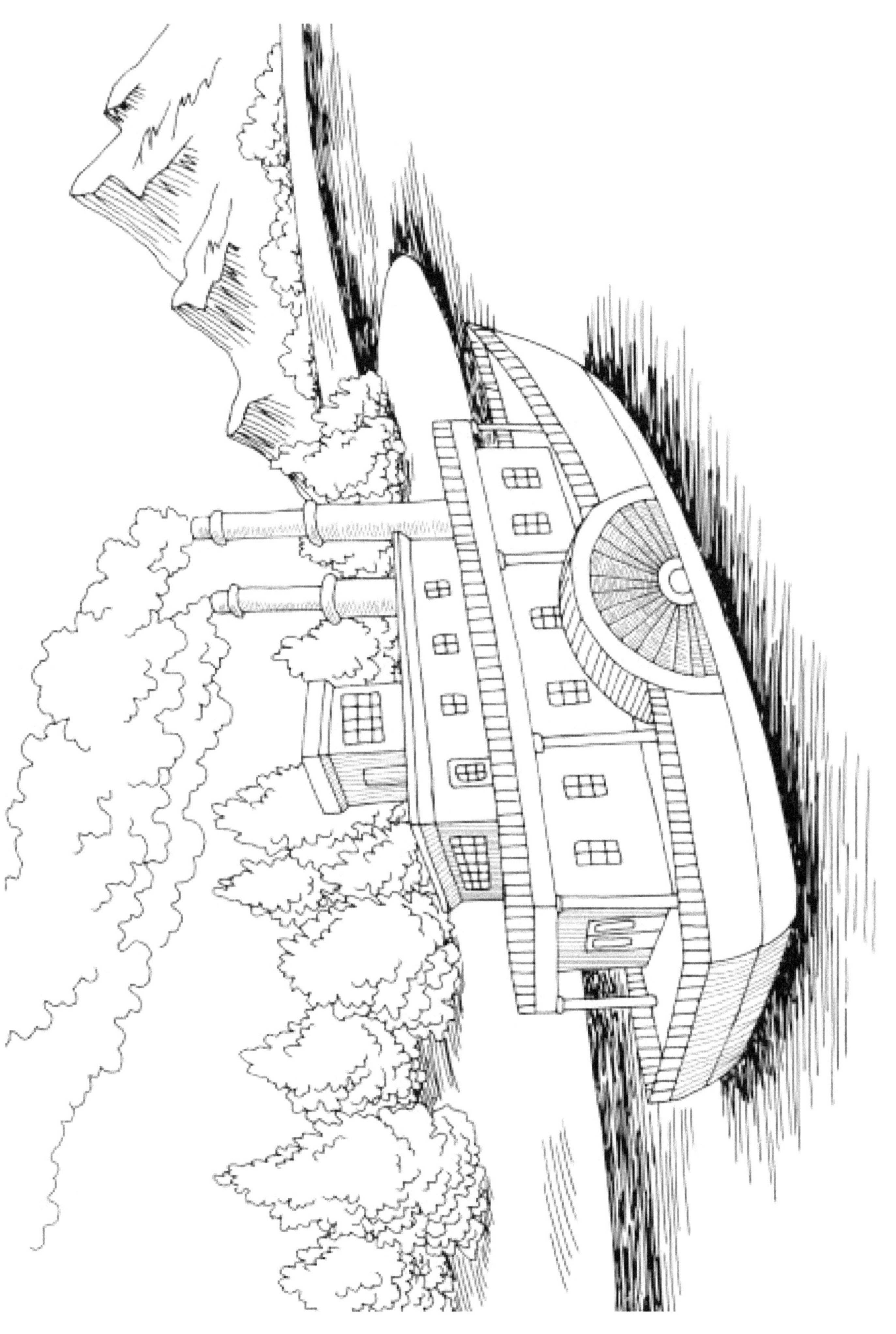

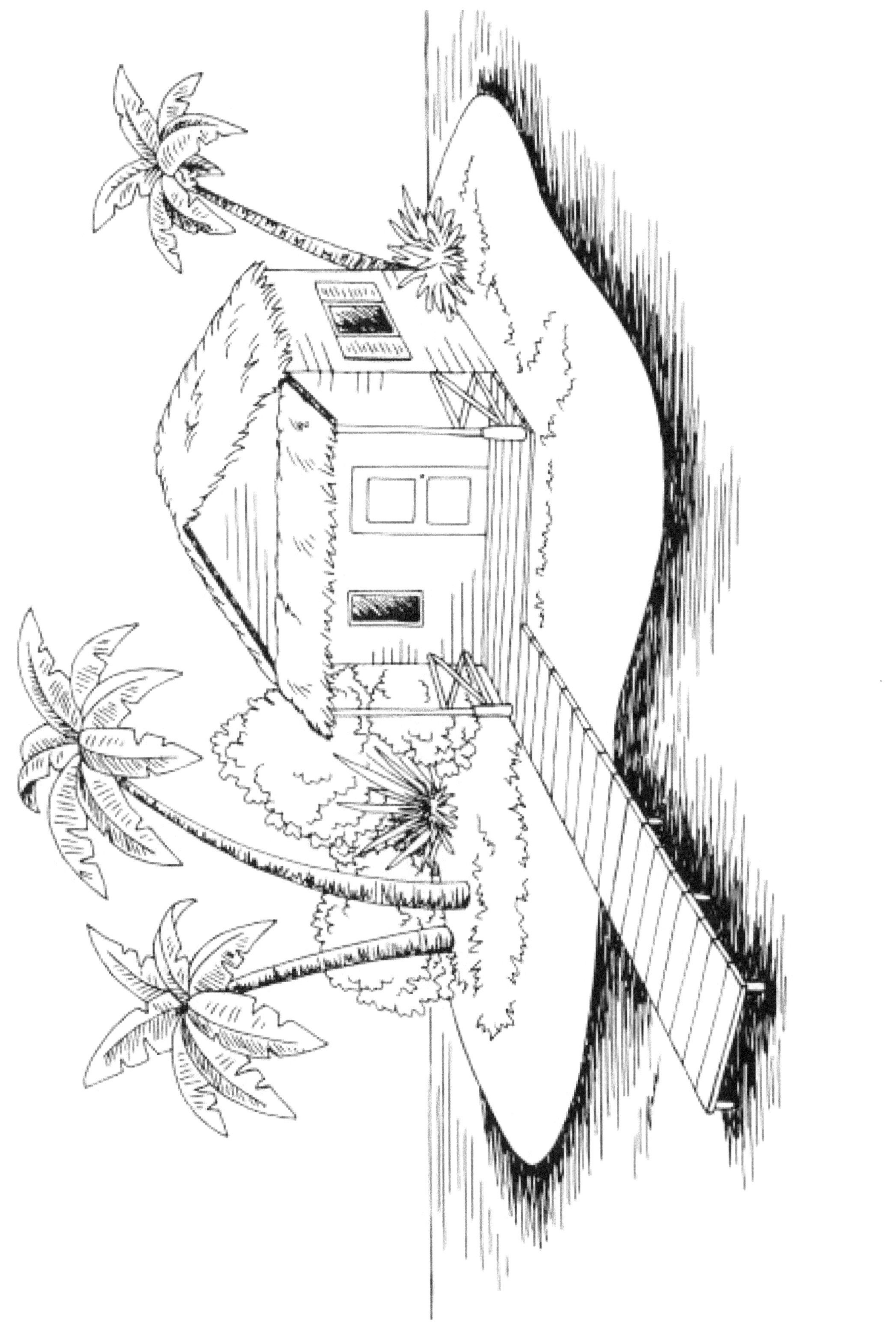

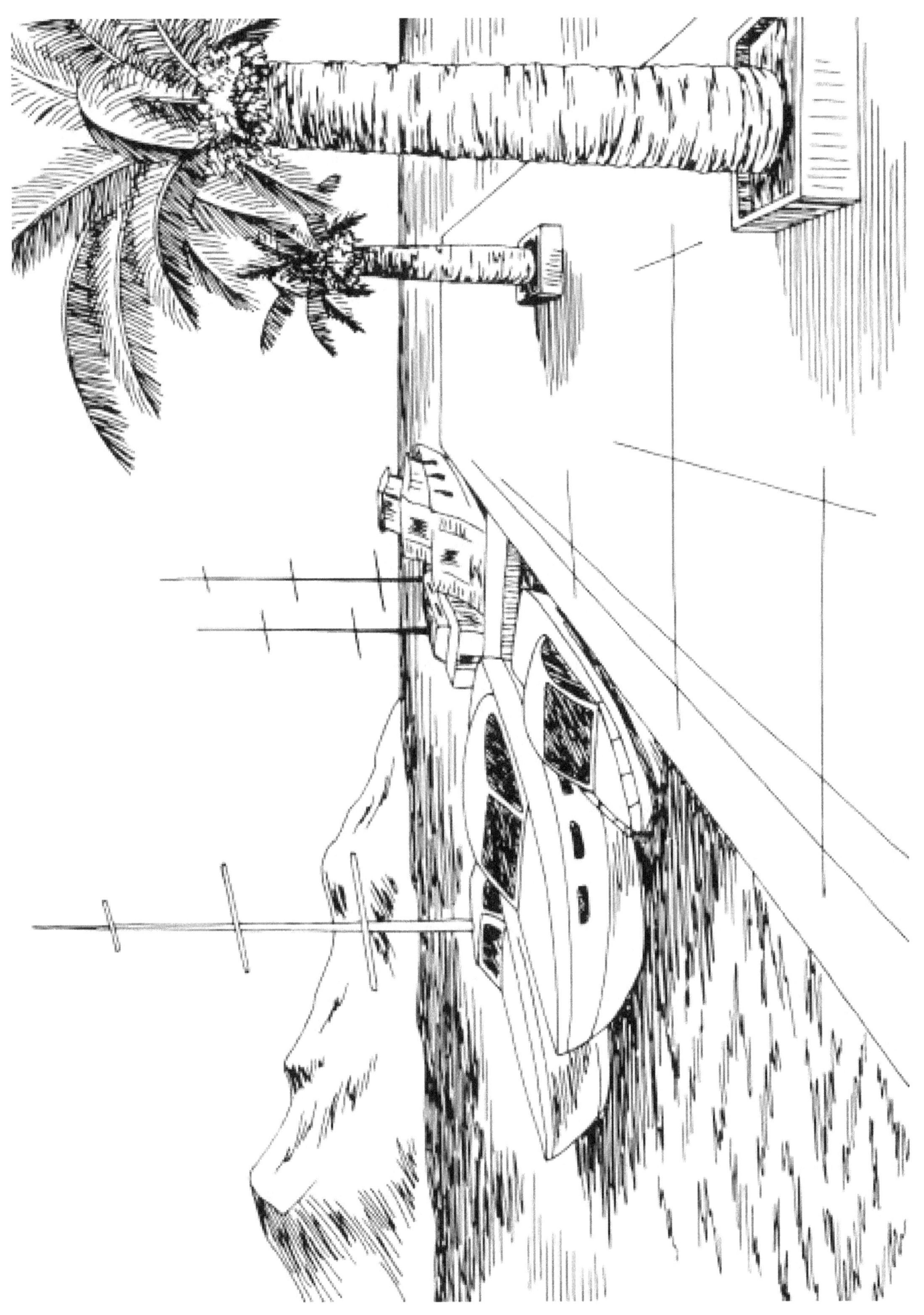

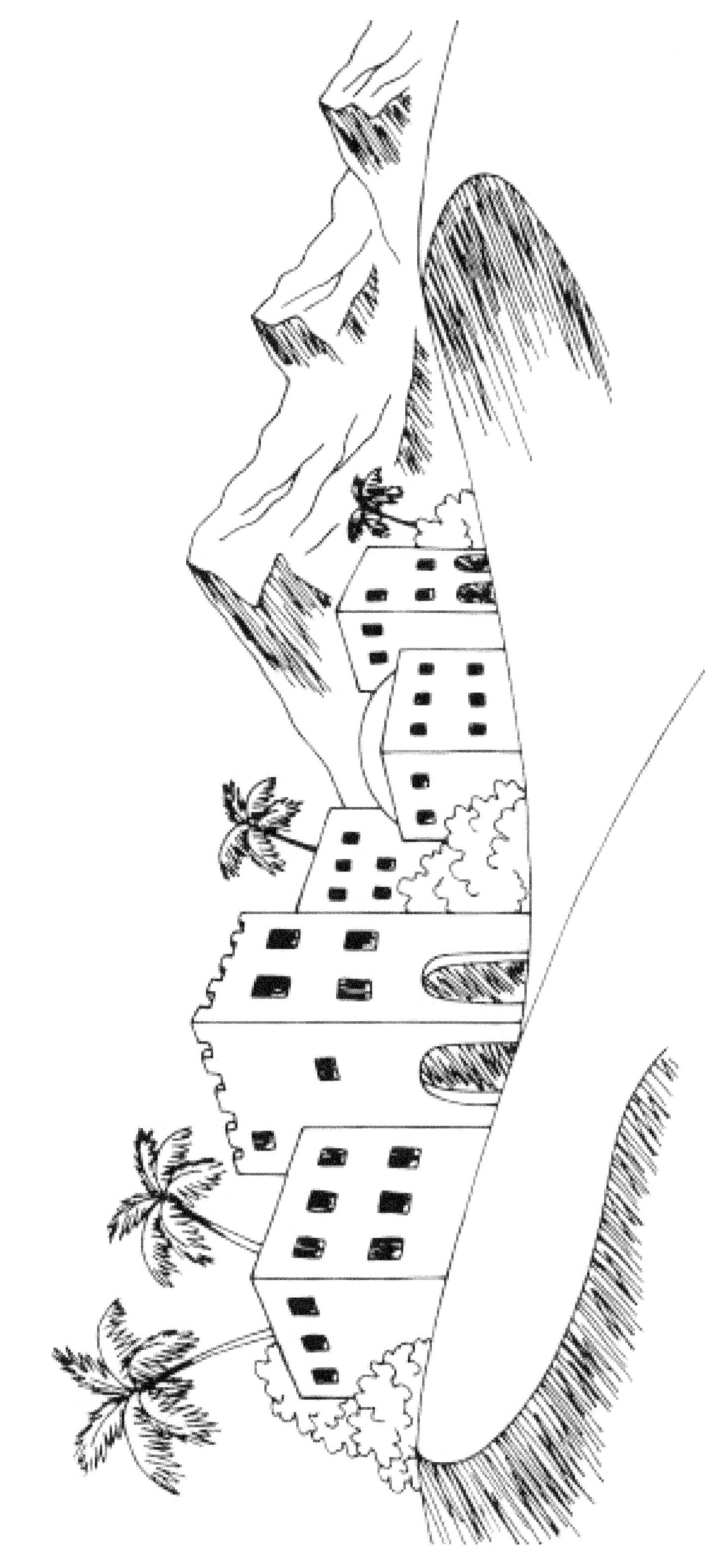

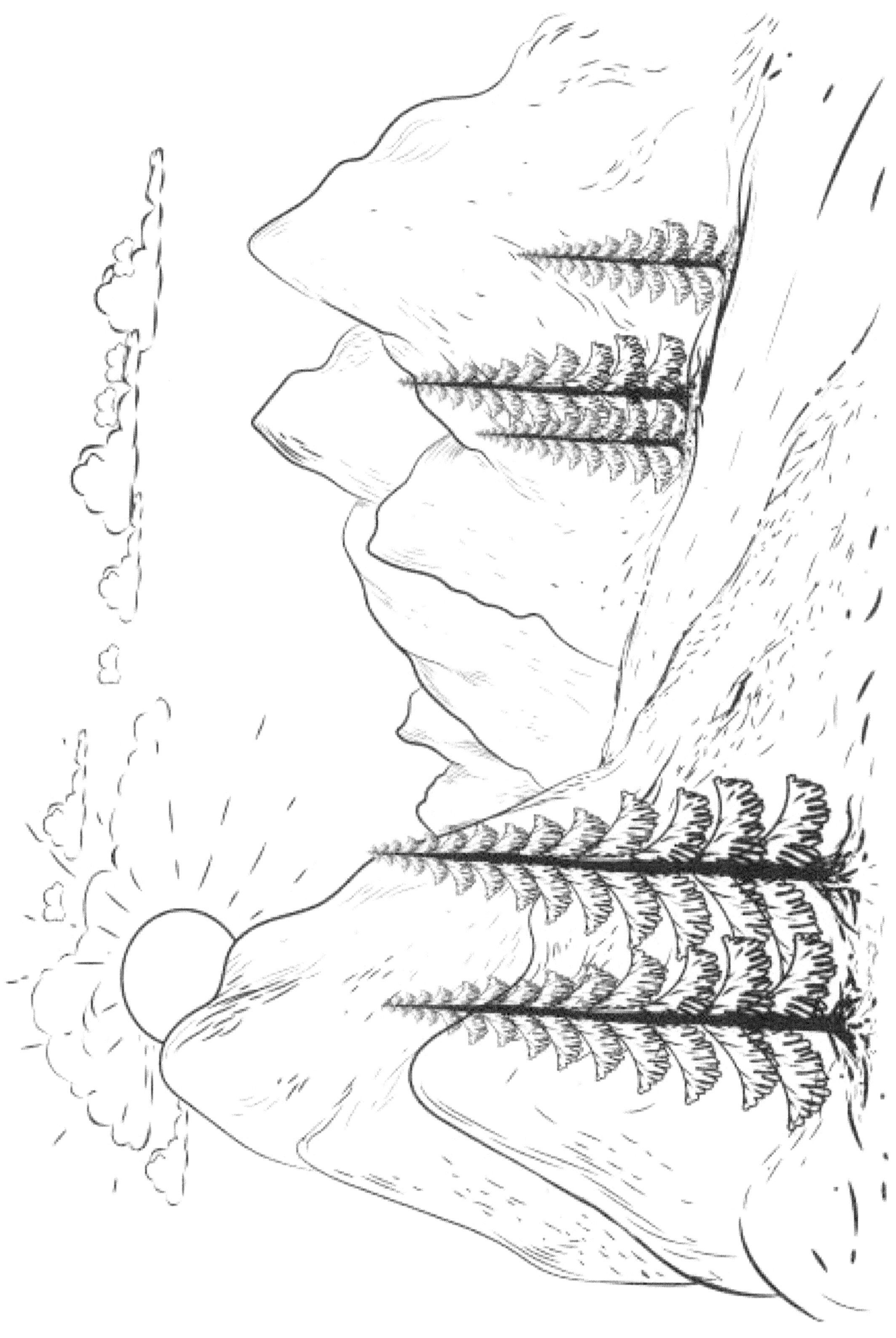

CONCLUSION

Thank you very much for buying this.
book.
If you enjoyed it, please leave a
Amazon review.
reviews are the soul
of our editorial efforts by leaving a
positive review would mean the world to us.